25

Science

MINI-BOOKS

Reproducible • Easy-To-Make • Easy-to-Read

by Esther Weiner

SCHOLASTIC
PROFESSIONAL BOOKS

NEW YORK • TORONTO • LONDON • AUCKLAND • SYDNEY

To the children of the E.M. Baker School
in Great Neck, New York

Designed by Jacqueline Swensen
Cover design by Vincent Ceci
Cover and interior illustration by Ellen Joy Sasaki

ISBN 0-590-49507-0

20 19 18 17 16 15 14 13 12   9/9 0 1 2 3/0

Copyright © 1994 by Esther B. Weiner   14

Printed in U.S.A.

TABLE OF CONTENTS

*Please note: **I recommend using the first starred lesson in each main section before you use the other mini-books in the section.** They are designed to provide a good basis for understanding all the other concepts covered.

   The order which follows the first lesson in each topic is logical, but it does not need to be adhered to for mastery of the concepts. Begin with any section you wish to.

3

INTRODUCTION

I consider myself to be very fortunate. I love every minute of my day, teaching hands-on science to kindergarten through fifth grade at the E. M. Baker School in Great Neck, New York. I am always looking for ways to improve and enhance my program, and this book is a direct outgrowth of that desire.

I encourage my students to predict, hypothesize, test and summarize their results in cooperative groups. I want my students to realize that hands-on science is not just tinkering with materials, but is a chance to discover that the natural world is really ruled by only a few scientific concepts. Mastery of those concepts leads to understanding of the world we live in. Careful record keeping and communication is vital so that findings and new knowledge can be transferred to many different situations.

Reading in the content area should be an accompaniment to hands-on science, but it is very difficult to devote time to both during the crowded school day, where you have so many curriculum challenges to meet. In my own teaching situation, it is next to impossible because of time constraints.

Yet I wish my students to develop the ability to read articles and be able to analyze them for their scientific information. I want them to develop the habit of reading magazines and newspapers for science content so that they can become scientifically literate citizens, who can make well-informed decisions as adults.

Of course, children in kindergarten through second grade (or even third grade) would have a very difficult time perusing the paper looking for science-related information, so it is for this reason that I have created this book of science concept mini-books.

Each mini-book was created with the desire to provide the young scientist with a motivating, informational reading adventure which illustrates an important science concept. I envision these mini-books as launches into the exploding world of scientific information.

Children enjoy the surprise of "peek-a-boo" cut and fold books, and this format is an enticing motivation to reading. I have purposely used simple designs which will enable you, the teacher, to spend more time with hands-on science and actual reading and less time instructing how to fold and cut.

Each mini-book can be used as a motivator or as a follow-up to a hands-on experience. The mini-books can be used as follow-up home-work reading to be shared with parents, as well.

Depending upon the grade you teach, you may either first read them together in small groups or use them as a whole class experience. I highly recommend children taking turns reading to each other, after you have familiarized them with an initial teacher-directed reading experience.

I have successfully used these books in grades higher than three, as well, to facilitate independent mastery of content and self-responsibility for learning. (See the Section on page 8 for specific activities to try with older students.)

Feel free to pick and choose from the selection; however, there are certain mini-books which should be read before others, to facilitate better understanding of their concepts. I have arranged the table of contents to clue you in as to what should be presented first.

I have included some "mini-lessons" for coordinating hands-on activities, as well as the precise science concept each mini-book was designed to communicate. For more specific hands-on experiences, please refer to my two other books, *Dirt Cheap Science* and *Cooperative Learning: Science Activities, Experiments, and Games.*

This project consumed several erasers during the planning stages—proving how useful friction can be! I hope you and your students enjoy using these mini-books as much as I have enjoyed creating them.

Esther Weiner

DIRECTIONS

MATERIALS NEEDED

These mini-books were designed to be interactive, and thus many of them require the use of crayons and pencil, besides a scissor.

Encourage the children to color each book realistically to enhance both the appearance and scientific content.

For your own peace of mind, make extra copies when you reproduce each booklet, and have a supply of invisible, non-glare tape available for repairs.

HELPFUL, BUT NOT NECESSARY MATERIALS

If you have access to glue sticks, a dot of glue placed between sections with NO information on them may be helpful when the children are actually reading and handling them. This is not a necessity, but it does make the mini-books a bit more sturdy. If you help your students understand that it is silly to glue things together that they want to read, they will quickly point out places that should be glued together.

Make a mini-book beforehand with one of the extras you copied. Experiment with the glue stick, so you know exactly where a dot of glue will help. (I did not put glue instructions on the mini-books themselves, because I felt that the additional words would only confuse beginning readers.)

REPRODUCING DIRECTIONS

1. Carefully remove the mini-book to be copied from the book, along the perforations.

2. If you are fortunate to have a copier which copies two-sided documents, press the button which states "two-sided original to two-sided copy".
Remember to make extra copies.

OR

2. If your copier only copies one side at a time, copy the title page side first (be extra sure to make extra copies), and then place the title page copies face down in the copy tray. The title should be in the right hand corner.

Copy the original mini-booklet's other side, with that side's print upside down on the glass platen. Print the same number of copies you originally made.

Always print one copy first to be sure that you've placed the paper in properly, and the booklet appears as you wish it to. To double check the mini-book, fold the copy to make sure everything is where it is supposed to be.

This can be frustrating the first few times you try this, but you will get better at it with practice.

3. Replace the original page back into the book, and secure with a paper clip for safe keeping.

PRESENTATION OF THE MINI-BOOKS AS A MINI-MYSTERY

I do not tell the children that they are going to make a mini-book. I always give them the reproduction and let them look at it for a moment. Someone always realizes that some of the words are upside down. They are intrigued by the strange appearance of the paper, and want to know why it is like that.

I tell them that it is a scientific mystery that they are going to solve, when they follow the directions, and watch me carefully.

Following of verbal and visual directions is a very important skill, and the very act of preparing these mini-books helps students refine it.

FOLDING AND CUTTING DIRECTIONS

(Be sure to model every step for your students.)

1. Have the children hold the page so that the side without the title page is facing them and placed flat upon their desks.

   Usually, the words should not be upside down. (In general, the side that faces them will have less information than the side with the title page.)

2. Have them fold the paper in half from top to bottom. Be sure to emphasize that the corners should meet or "kiss." At this point, they should see pages 2 and 3.

   With very young children, I find that it is important to stress that two hands be used for the folding, and that the paper should be flat upon their desks.

   You may have to show them how to crease a paper, in addition to folding it.

3. Be sure the children now see only pages 2 and 3.

   They then should fold from side to side, so only the title page or page 4 is visible.

4. Hold up your copy, showing them the title page, and instruct them to place the booklet upon their desk, with only the title visible.

   At this point, I always have my students write their names upon the title page, because they are making a "special present" that they will want to keep safe.

   (At this point, someone will excitedly realize that they are making a little book.)

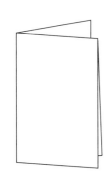

5. Ask the children to unfold their booklets. (I always inform them that they shouldn't worry, because the books know how to refold themselves again.)

6. Cutting takes place ONLY on the solid lines. (Folding takes place on the dotted lines.) You may find it helpful to demonstrate the cutting of each page and then having the class do that page, immediately after you model it.

7. Have the students refold the booklet, reminding them that the book already knows how to fold itself up. (I usually hold the book up in the air from its bottom edge,

showing them that the top falls down to refold itself.

Some recreasing may be needed, particularly where there are flaps.

8. As the children read through the book, they can fold the flaps to reveal the surprises and answers. (There are always squeals of delight.)

USING THESE BOOKS WITH PRE-READING CHILDREN

Try to use the suggested mini-lessons printed within the text to familiarize the children with the concepts covered by the books.

When I use the books with children who cannot read independently, we sit in small groups, and I read aloud and demonstrate the opening and closing of the flaps.

Then I read the book again and leave out words that they might recognize, allowing them to call out the missing word.

Finally, I pair children who have more skill in reading with those less skilled, and I invite them to share the books together.

Of course, the ultimate beauty of the mini-books is that they can be taken home and read with parents for reinforcement in reading, and science concepts.

FOR GRADES TWO AND ABOVE: COOPERATIVE LEARNING ACTIVITIES AND STUDY SKILLS

Don't be afraid to use mini-books with older students. They react with pleasure to them, and this positive response will enable you to introduce study skills in a painless, pleasant way.

You can make the books even more interactive for older students by following these suggestions:

"Bump" up the books for more advanced students, by inviting them to add information to the books by themselves. For instance, in the Plant Parts Mini-book, students can add information about the jobs of roots to both the title page and page two. They can add more mature vocabulary to the flap on page three dealing with stems. (Pipes in stems are called xylem, and the word can be written on the long arrow.)

Encourage your students in second grade and above to become more responsible for their own retention of facts, by playing the "Be the Teacher" Game.

Have the students write three questions pertaining to the mini-book they have read, and place the answers to the questions on the back of the question sheet.

Each student works with a partner by exchanging their questions and trying to write an answer, or verbally answer it.

Then the students work as a cooperative group of four by exchanging papers further and deciding which is the best question from the four papers.

That child gets to stand up, ask the class the question, and select the student who answers it.

You can use an activity such as this to demonstrate how to frame questions, and how to devise questions which require more in-depth answers. (I always ask my students to "explain" the reasons for their answers.)

Try to pair use of the mini-books with either the mini-lessons included, or with some of the very inexpensive, easy to follow lessons in *Dirt Cheap Science* or *Cooperative Learning*:

Science Activities, Experiments, and Games or any science texts used in your school.
The books CAN be used without hands-on activities, as well.

ADDITIONAL ADVANTAGES OF SCIENCE MINI-BOOKS

Unfortunately, there are many children who do not have books in their homes. Using mini-books is a cost-effective way of giving them a book that they can own and read with a reading partner.

If you present the books with enthusiasm, the children will receive them as a valuable treasure.

The scientific subject matter is easily grasped by a more mature reader, so the mini-book can be discussed while it is being read at home.

Our hope is that having mini-books in the home will encourage families to visit the library and increase their children's exposure to books in general.

CONCEPTS AND MINI-LESSONS

LIFE SCIENCE

PLANT PARTS

(Mini-book on Page 23)

Concept: Plants are systems because their parts work together. Each part has a specific function and adaptation which enables the entire plant to survive.

This concept can and should be generalized to include animal life.

Mini-lesson:

1. Go on a weeding expedition to uproot plants and examine their root systems.

2. Try the old food coloring and water trick with celery stems to see water travel up to the leaves.

3. Place a water plant such as elodea in a small, covered test tube to see it produce bubbles of oxygen that fish can breathe.

WHAT ARE FLOWERS FOR?

(Mini-book on page 25)

Concept: Flowers and small animals interact and depend upon each other in ecosystems. Animals help flowers produce seeds for the continuation of the plant's life cycle, and flowers provide food to animals.

Flowers are systems whose parts function together.

Mini-lesson:

1. Get hold of some "perfect" flowers—that is, flowers with both male and female reproductive parts of stamen and pistil. Provide sketching materials, and after the sketching occurs, dissect the flowers to see their parts.

2. Go on an ecology walk to see other insects interacting with flowers and to hypothesize how the wind can help flowers. (Pollination by wind occurs in most tree flowers and is responsible for the coughing and sneezing that takes place every spring!)

WHAT'S A SEED?

(Mini-book on page 27)

Concept: Seeds contain embryo plants, and food to sustain the embryo until it is able to produce its own food. Seeds continue the life cycle of plants and also are a vital part of food chains.

Mini-lesson:

1. Soak lima beans overnight, and have the children dissect them to find the embryo plant inside.

2. Make peanut butter after opening peanuts to find their embryo plants.

3. Go on a seed hunt outdoors to find many different kinds of seeds. Classify them into groups and count them to have the class realize that many more seeds are produced than actually grow. Brainstorm a list of animals which might eat them.

SEEDS ON THE GO!

(Mini-book on page 29)

Please note: This book unfolds, rather than having flaps.

Concept: Seeds must disperse to suitable environments so they can grow to maturity. Dispersal depends upon either animals or wind, and seeds have developed adaptations to take advantage of these "travel agents."

Mini-lesson:

1. Go on a "seed hunt" to discover the many different kinds of seeds there are.

    If you have old socks, children can put them over their shoes, to see if any seeds "hitchhike" on them.

    (This mini-book does not mention hitchhiker seeds, which are any seeds with points or hooks that ride on animals which are not aware that they are helping them disperse.)

2. Count and classify the seeds the class finds. A picto-graph with glued on seeds can be used to record information.

FOOD CHAINS

(Mini-book on page 31)

Concept: A food chain is a hierarchy of eaters, using energy which is passed along from the sun.

All food chains consist of a consumer (eater) and a producer of food (green plant). Carnivores eat animals which may be other carnivores, or herbivores. Herbivores eat plants. Plants manufacture their own food through the process of photosynthesis using carbon dioxide and water, with sunlight for the energy to create sugar from those non-living ingredients. Green plants are the only living things which can manufacture their own food using the sun's energy.

Mini-lesson:

1. Have the children recall what they ate during the day and trace back to see the members of their food chains.

2. Second graders and up can research an animal to create a mobile with illustrated pictures of the animal's food chain.

3. What would happen to the animal if a member of its food chain disappeared? What would happen if sunlight was blocked from Earth by pollution (from volcanic eruptions, for example)?

    Most students should realize that members of food chains depend upon each other and the sun for their energy.

4. Discuss an animal that is feared for its predatory ways—such as a shark. Why do we need sharks and other "scary" animals?

    (The populations of animals in the lower parts of the food chain would become too large, and those animals would starve and die anyway.)

    The point is, every member of a food chain is valuable, and even if we don't particularly like the "ways" of an animal, it has an important purpose in the ecosystem.

11

EATING FOR ENERGY

(Mini-book on page 33)

Concept: Animals are adapted for eating certain types of food; the human body consists of parts that work together in systems, and these systems work together to help us survive.

Digestion consists of breaking food down into molecular size so its energy may be accessed by the animal's entire body.

Mini-lesson:

1. Have the children look at their teeth in mirrors to identify molars with their many cusps, and the cutting edges of incisors. Challenge them to eat something at home only using their incisors for chewing.

2. Ask what saliva is for.

   Hand out saltine crackers, and have the students place a small piece in their mouth, and let it sit there in the saliva. (Saliva chemically breaks down starches into simpler sugars, besides wetting food to make it easier to swallow.)

3. To simulate the peristaltic action of the esophagus, challenge the children to squeeze a tennis ball down a stocking within 7 seconds.

4. To simulate a stomach, place old, unwanted food into a small, plastic bag, and mash it up, using their hands as a model for the stomach's muscular action.

5. Have children act as the parts of the digestive system, tearing a piece of paper into smaller pieces as it travels through. Then have students act as blood, picking up the molecules of food, and deliver them to other students who will be cells in the rest of the body.

CLEAN IS HEALTHY!

(MIni-book on page 35)

Concept: Germs and bacteria are too small to be seen without the use of a microscope, but their spread and the illnesses they cause can be prevented through proper hygienic behavior.

Mini-lesson:

1. Practice simple first aid by placing a dot of red, **washable** marker on a "victim's" finger, and then having the child wash the dot off carefully, using soap and water, and then apply a band-aid.

   Discuss the importance of bike helmets, protective clothing, skateboard pads, and of course, seatbelts to prevent injuries which can tear the skin.

THE POND COMMUNITY

(Mini-book on page 37)

Concept: A community is a group of plants and animals living and depending upon each other in the same physical environment.

Mini-lesson:

1. Visit local ponds to observe plant and animal life.

2. Construct food chains which might exist in pond areas. Challenge the children to connect the food chains to create pond food webs.

12

3. Build 3-d models of ponds and their community members, using shoeboxes.

4. If your budget permits, create a terrarium pond, with small turtles, fish, and plant life.

READING A BIRD
(Mini-book on page 39)

Concept: Animals have adaptations (properties) which enable them to survive in their environment by making a living and escaping predators with a variety of strategies.

By "reading" a bird to examine its feathers, claws and feet, it is possible to know what kind of eater it is and where it lives. Observing adaptations of animals, in general, can give good clues to their living habits.

Mini-lesson:

1. Go bird watching to observe beak shapes, and claws. Look at colors of birds, and ask why so many seem to be browns, or grays. Have the children observe the behavior of the birds.

2. Dyed feathers can easily be purchased from arts and crafts suppliers. Have each child compare small down feathers to larger flight feathers by holding one in each hand, and pushing against the air with them. Which would help push against the air and provide lift better? Which would provide warmth?

Have the children make one hand into a beak with the thumb and fingers opposing.

Have them unzip (separate the barbs) a flight feather to clean and preen it, as a bird would, and then have them rezip it, to see how the barbs of feathers are like velcro.

3. Extend the idea of physical adaptations into behavioral adaptations. Have the children notice when birds seem to sing the most. (At dusk, and at sunrise, to establish their territories.)

LIFE CYCLES
(Mini-book on page 41)

Concept: Animals and plants have patterns of birth and development to maturity so they can reproduce themselves. This pattern is called a life cycle.

While it may seem that life cycles in plants and animals are very different, in fact, they are both sexual. Plants make eggs and sperm (in pollen). Pollination and fertilization may use different methods in different species, but it is still sexual.

Some animals take great care of their young, while other animals birth their young, and that is where their responsibility ends. In general, the less care given to young means that more young must be born at one time.

Plants are highly prolific in creating seeds, and insects, for instance, have huge numbers of offspring at a time.

Mini-lesson:

1. You can use this mini-book to launch a discussion of families, and why humans do not have so many babies at a time. (To enable parents to provide the proper type of care.)

2. Research the number of years species need to grow to maturity, and graph it on a bar graph. Is there a relationship between the time necessary for maturity, and the number of young a species produces at a time? Why?

HOME IS

(Mini-book on page 43)

Concept: Animals depend upon plants for their shelter; creation of a home is an instinctive behavioral adaptation.

An instinct is a behavior which animals are born knowing, to help them survive in their environment.

Mini-lesson:

1. Have the children create their own nests, using shoeboxes and collecting plant materials birds might use. The shoebox can hold the nest, as they fashion it by weaving straw and twigs together. Use white glue to help hold the nest together.

    This will be difficult but fun to do. Ask the children if birds go to school to learn how to make their homes. (They are born with the knowledge of how to do it. This is called instinct, and it helps animals survive by knowing how to behave.

2. Ask if humans have any instincts. Did the children have to go to school to learn how to cry? What purpose does crying serve for a baby's survival?

3. Create spider webs by giving yarn to students, and inviting them to work in cooperative pairs tying string to their adjoining chairs, instead of trees.

HIDE AND SEEK

(Mini-book on page 45)

Concept: Camouflage is an adaptation which helps animals both escape their predators, and escape detection from those they are hunting for food.

Another adaptation similar to camouflage is that of mimicry. For example, butterflies may look as if they have huge eyes on their wings. This is to frighten away predators by tricking them into thinking the eyes belong to something that may eat them!

Mini-lesson:

1. Have the class create a mural of a forest scene, for example. Then have children research the animals in the forest community, and draw, color and place them in their proper camouflaged place.

2. Research animals in other communities such as jungles. When we see animals in traditional zoo settings, sometimes animals do not seem to be camouflaged—when you see a tiger in a cage, it doesn't seem possible it could blend into the background. Stripes help animals blend into sunlit high grasses. The darker stripes seem like shadows.

    How would spots help an animal? (In the case of a leopard, they help them hide in dappled sunlight in the treetops' leaves.)

    How could brightly colored birds blend in? (They are mimicking brightly colored flowers.)

3. How can being brightly colored help an animal survive? Research why ladybugs are brightly colored. (This color signals birds that these insects will taste terrible. After trying one, birds will avoid other insects with those colors! What other insects use survival adaptations such as these?)

NATURE AT NIGHT

(Mini-book on page 47)

Concept: Some animals prey on their food at night.

Mini-lesson:

1. Have the children read the mini-book and then brainstorm as many reasons as they can for animals to be active at night.

2. Rent nature videos which show nocturnal animals. Freeze-frame them, and have the children "read" the animal to discover the adaptations which enable the animal to be nocturnal.

    The mini-book does not explain the adaptations of a barn owl, so here is some background:

    Owls have huge ear openings hidden under their feathers, to enable them to hear their prey. Their feathers are incredibly soft, so they are not noisy—avoiding tipping off prey that they are present and avoiding interfering with their hearing. Their large eyes are not used for sighting prey, so much as for avoiding crashing into objects as they fly in pursuit of their dinners.

3. Call the local zoo to see if there are nocturnal animals on display in naturalized settings. Try to arrange a visit, or send home a letter to parents giving information about the zoo's exhibit.

EARTH SCIENCE

PLANET EARTH; A RIDDLE BOOK!

(Mini-book on page 49)

Concept: Earth has three major parts: a crust, mantle, and core. The crust is made of huge plates that move over the mantle.

Mini-lesson:

1. Make some pudding. (Do not use the instant kind.) Have the children observe the change of state from liquid to solid, as it cools off. Which part cools off fastest? Which part gets the hardest? (The skin of the pudding, which can be likened to how the Earth's crust formed.)

    Which part is the thinnest?

    (Again, the skin, which is like the Earth's extremely thin crust-which at most is 35 miles deep, and at its thinnest under the oceans, where it can be only 5-7 miles thick.)

    Why do you have to wait to eat the pudding, even if the pudding skin is cool? (Because the inner part is still too warm.)

    The part underneath the skin can be likened to the Earth's molten mantle. It will never harden either!

    Enjoy eating the crust and mantle pudding!

2. Bake some cookies. Have the children observe the cracks which form as the crust of the cookies cools off. These cracks can represent the Earth's faults, which formed in pretty much the same way: by cooling off.

Have the students break the cookies along the fault lines, and then put them back together like a puzzle to form a "whole" Earth.

Complete the lesson by chewing up both plates and faults.

S-L-O-W CHANGES ON EARTH

(Mini-book on page 51)

Concept: The Earth's crust changes as a result of movement energy travelling through it from the motion of magma within the mantle.

Mini-lesson:

1. Make a model of the Earth's mantle and crust in a transparent container. Use red tinted water to represent the hot mantle. Cut a styrofoam plate into a few pieces and place on top of the water to represent the Earth's plates. (They should be re-aligned like a puzzle put together again.)

   Have the children stand around the desk the model is on and stamp their feet to simulate the movement of magma within the mantle. This will cause the plates to shift around slightly.

   (Test it out yourself to make sure you didn't cut in such a way as to prevent any observable movement of the plates.)

   The Earth's plates only move about 2 inches a year, so use that fact to explain that they shouldn't be disappointed in the lack of exciting motion from their stamping feet.

   Sometimes the plates "stick" together, building up tremendous pressure until finally it is released in the form of plate movement called an earthquake. The vibrations travel through the ground, passing energy along, causing tremendous damage, depending upon the type of soil, and amount of development which has taken place in the area.

   Earthquakes emanate from fault-lines.

2. To demonstrate erosion, fill small containers with either soil or sand. Let the children create rain by using water droppers, and observing how the water carries soil to a different part of the container.

   You (the teacher) should demonstrate erosion by wind by blowing gently upon the surface of the soil. (This avoids children blowing soil into each other's faces!)

3. Take an erosion walk after a strong rainfall to observe how soil is washed onto sidewalks and into places it is not normally seen.

   Where does the soil end up?

   (It should be at lower elevations, and the children should realize that the rain and the Earth's gravity washed it down.)

PLAYING WITH EARTH'S GRAVITY

(Mini-book on page 53)

Concept: Gravity is an unseen force that pulls everything on earth towards the center of the earth.

Mini-lesson:

1. Challenge the children to stand up, put their hands at their sides and jump "up."

   When they come down, pretend to be annoyed because they did not listen to you. You told them to jump "up." Why didn't they listen?

16

Read the mini-book, and then talk about the force that pulls everything to the earth—gravity.

Invite the students to hold their hands up, and not put them down. Have them keep them up until they begin to groan and complain. Ask why their hands were so tired. (Gravity is pulling on them.)

2. Go out on the playground to observe equipment, and analyze whether or not gravity plays a part in the way it works.

3. Why is it easier to go down the stairs rather than up?

A TRIP IN SPACE ON SPACESHIP EARTH (TIME)
(Mini-book on page 55)
Mini-lesson:

1. Place a large ball or large yellow paper sun in the center of the room. Place signs with each month chronologically around the room. Each child should begin where their birthday month is and walk in the same direction to orbit the sun. A year will have passed when they complete their orbit and get back to where they started.

2. If you are using this booklet around New Year's, have each child say "Happy New Year" when they pass the sign that says January.

3. Read the *Connect the Dots* (Constellations) mini-book. Then you can point out that they will have a different view of the star scenery as they take their trip through space through the year, just like the scenery changes when they take a ride in the car. That's one way we know when we have completed another year's trip around the sun.
   What other clues tell us that a trip has been completed?
   (Discuss the cycle of the seasons.)

TAKE A SPIN ON PLANET EARTH (TIME)
(Mini-book on page 57)
Mini-lesson:

1. If you have flashlights, let the children work in small groups to conduct the following demonstration, or set up a lamp without a lampshade to be a model for the sun. Invite each child to come up and be the Earth. Their nose is where they live, and the back of their head is the other side of the Earth.
   Each child should have a chance to rotate, facing into and away from the "sun" to understand that it is the spinning of the Earth that causes day and night to occur.

2. To demonstrate that why we don't see stars during the daylight is due to "camouflage" from the sun's brilliant light, turn a flashlight on (this works better with weaker batteries) and aim it on the ceiling. Turn the lights off, and ask if it looks brighter or dimmer. (Of course, it will appear brighter when the lights are off, and will dim when the lights are on.)
   The children should now be able to hypothesize why we don't see as many stars when it is a full moon. (Moonlight also camouflages starlight.)

3. Use this mini-book to launch a study of the calendar. Review the "A Trip On Spaceship Earth" book so the children realize that the Earth both revolves around the sun and rotates while that is happening.

CONNECT THE DOTS! A STARRY STORY OF CONSTELLATIONS
(Mini-book on page 59)
Mini-lesson:

1. After reading this mini-book, gather seven flashlights, and choose seven children to hold them. They can try to recreate a dipper on the ceiling of the classroom by conferring with each other to decide which star they will project.

   Select other children to try and recreate Orion (minus the star in his head because it is not really visible easily to us).

2. Allow children to create their own constellations, using foil stars on black paper or chalk on black paper. Challenge them to create a story or myth about their stars and then tell it to their cooperative partner, or commit it to paper.

EARTH, PLANET # 3 (SOLAR SYSTEM)
(Mini-book on page 61)
Mini-lesson:

1. Using the center of the room as the sun, select children to be "planets" which orbit around.

2. This mini-book can be used in conjunction with the "Pond Community" mini-book to launch a discussion for Earth Day, or a unit in ecology. Use the mini-book to illustrate the precarious position we are in—we live on the only planet which can support life, so we'd better take care of it.

PHYSICAL SCIENCE

BIG AND LITTLE MATTER
(Mini-book on page 63)
Mini-lesson:
Hint: Try these activities before reading the mini-book.

1. To establish the fact that all matter takes up room, invite a student to sit on a chair. Invite another student to sit upon the same chair, at the same time. Inform them that they may not share the chair at all. Can it be done? Scientifically speaking, it is impossible, because two objects cannot be in the same place at the same time.

   Ask what happens when two cars try to be in the same exact place at the same time.

2. To show that a smaller object can block out a larger one, have the children focus upon a chart on the wall. Have them bring their hand in front of their eyes. Why is the larger chart blocked out? (The close hand, though smaller, appears larger than the faraway chart.)

   Of course, this demonstration can explain why the moon looks larger than stars or the sun and why it is able to block out the sun during a solar eclipse, or why mommy looks so small when she is down the block!

3. To demonstrate that objects can be so small that they are invisible, show the children a grain of sand, and then place it across the room from them, while they hide their eyes. Challenge them to find it. After they have trouble locating it, inform them that all matter is made of even smaller particles than the grain of sand. I introduce the terms *molecule* and *atom* in my kindergarten classes, and they manage them with as much ease as they would the word *particle*.

Relate this concept of matter being made of small molecules, to their building experiences with little "legos."

You can make very big, interesting structures with little, tiny building blocks.

Inform the children that all objects which take up room are called "matter." Why are they examples of matter?

WHY YOU CAN STAND ON A CHAIR (CHANGES OF MATTER)

(Mini-book on page 65)

Mini-lesson:

Prerequisite: Big and Little Matter Mini-book

1. Have the children act out a "Molecule Play". If you divide the class into three equal groups, each group can demonstrate molecules when arranged as a gas, liquid and solid.

When the "solid" group is in front of the class, they should be standing so close together that they have their arms on each other's shoulders. You (the teacher) should try to walk through them. (Of course, you should not be able to do so, because they are too close together.)

I always try to make my point about molecules holding tightly to each other, by trying to leave by walking through the closed door. It's worth the "bang" to make the point in a "silly" way.

When the liquid group comes up, they should touch hands, but not grab onto each other. You can then walk through them, but they rejoin hands as soon as you pass through. Be sure to ask if this is what happens when you move through water. (The water molecules rejoin each other as you pass through.)

When the gas group is on stage, you can simply "waltz" right through their wide open spaces. They don't hold hands or touch.

Which way was it easier to get through the molecules? Why is it easy to walk through the air? (It's a gas.) How do you know that air is made out of molecules if you can't see them?

(You can feel them when they are moving in a breeze, or you are moving against them.)

If there was a race between a person in a swimming pool and a person next to it, who would win? (The person moving through the air, because the molecules wouldn't hold him back.)

2. Make a classification chart of liquids, solids and gases found in the classroom.

3. Mix up a liquid and solid to release a gas: Place a teaspoon of baking soda into a small, clear container of vinegar. The resulting bubbles are carbon dioxide gas which is escaping the chemical system.

4. Do some baking to change liquids and solids and carbon dioxide gas released during

baking into a new type of matter: cake! (Baking soda or powder reacts to release CO_2, so the cake will be fluffy, rather than leaden.)

5. Place a spoon into a clear glass of water fresh from the tap.

Air bubbles will begin to cling to it, showing that air (a gas) is also found in water. How does that help fish and other water animals? (It provides the oxygen that they need.)

CLOUDS (THE WATER CYCLE)

(Mini-book on page 67)
Mini-lesson:

1. Make a mini-water cycle by placing a small amount of water into a clear, sealed plastic baggie. Hang it in the sunlight and watch the water condense upon the walls of the bag after it evaporates. It will then rain down the walls of the bag, creating a cycle.

2. If it is possible, boil some water in a pyrex pot, so the children can see the water bubbling. (This shows that the molecules are really jumping.)

I ask the children how they feel when they walk upon a hot beach. Do they walk slowly and heavily, or do they jump lightly across it? How would they feel if they were on the stove—would they stand still, or jump up to get out of the heat?

3. Build a terrarium using recycled soda bottles. Cut the top off the bottle and keep the cap on it. Place small pebbles in the bottom of the container, place a layer of top soil on that, plant some small plants which like a humid environment in the soil, and water the soil. Cap the terrarium with the top of the bottle.

The plants' leaves will transpire unwanted water into the air, and it will rain down the sides of the terrarium. (You will have to occasionally replenish some water, because this is not a totally sealed environment.)

4. The next time it rains, find a puddle and time how long it takes for it to evaporate. What kind of weather conditions were present? Compare it to other days with puddles of the same size. What makes the water molecules jump out of the puddle? (Sunlight and windy conditions make evaporation happen most rapidly.)

5. Invite students to paint the board with water in carefully measured areas. What ways can they brainstorm to help their spot evaporate fastest? (Fanning or holding a light near it are some suggestions.) **Please note: If you use a lightbulb as a model sun, the teacher should be the *only* person to hold the lamp.

You can run the evaporation contest either by timing the rate, or by "racing" directly against each other in areas on the board.

HEARING SOUNDS

(Mini-book on page 69)
Mini-lesson:

1. Hold a ruler up in front of the class so they can see it.

Ask if it is making a sound. (No.)

Place the ruler half on and half-off a desk. Push down on the free end and release it.

(Now it makes a sound.) Have the children observe what the ruler is doing as it produces the sound. (It is moving back and forth quickly—in other words, it is vibrating.)

What does an object have to do in order to produce a sound?
(It must be moving.)

2. To demonstrate how sound travels through the air, have children be molecules again. They should stand with shoulders touching lightly near each other in a line facing the class.

   You (the teacher) are the ruler. You touch a student at the end of the molecule line by shaking your shoulders back and forth in a vibrating motion, re-enacting the motion of the ruler. When that student feels your vibration, she starts to vibrate. The students should all begin to "vibrate" as they feel it passed along down the line.

3. To see how big ears really do catch sounds better, have students gently bend their outer ears forward. (Be sure they don't shut their ears closed.)

   They should hear sound slightly louder when they are flapped forward.

   You can also create "ear cones" out of construction paper, to try to catch more sounds.

4. To see that two ears help us hear in all directions, have a student stand in front of the class. Have them close their eyes, and you should snap your fingers in different places around their head. They will be able to tell you the number of fingersnaps, no matter where your hand was. Ask the children if this would happen if you were testing eyesight. Can you see in all directions?

5. To show what happens to sound once it travels through the ear canal, have the students construct an ear drum and canal model using an empty toilet paper roll, rubber band and piece of waxed paper large enough to cover one end of the paper tube. Use the rubber band to hold the waxed paper in place on the tube.

   Have one student whisper into the uncovered end (this is the ear opening), and have another student lightly place a finger upon the waxed paper. The paper will vibrate like an eardrum.

   You can use the delicacy of the waxed paper to explain why ears are so delicate and must be treated with respect. Objects should never be placed into ears, and it is very important to avoid loud music and earphones which are turned up too high. Not only are eardrums damaged, but the tiny hairs which must vibrate within the cochlea to turn sound energy into electrical energy get damaged.

   Have students act as the tiny bones in the ears and pass the vibrations along, in a "drama" similar to the molecule play in step 2. You may wish to have each participant hold a sign naming the bones in the inner ear. The child who is the cochlea can hold a string and a container of water which represents the fluid in the cochlea. A child who plays the brain can hold the other end of the string. The string represents the auditory nerve which carries the sound message to the brain.

LIGHT
(Mini-book on page 71)
Mini-lesson:

1. Before reading the mini-book, get hold of some prisms or diffraction paper. Have the students place them in the sun or shine a flashlight on them.

   What colors come out of the prism? What color is the light that goes in? (It does not appear to have any color except white when it goes in, but many colors go out.)

2. Ask what happens to a car when lots of sunlight goes into it. (It gets warm.) What does the light change into? Why is it a good idea to keep shades down in the house during the summer? (The light changes to heat when it gets inside.)

3. Why is it important to keep plants in the sunlight? (They use the sunlight for energy to "cook" their food. You may wish to have the students reread their *Plant Parts* mini-books at this point.)

Raise some seedlings from soaked lima beans in separate containers. When you have green plants, place half in a dark closet and keep the other half in the sunlight. Have the children predict what will happen, record their observations, and hypothesize that plants in the dark starve because they cannot make food without light energy.

4. Have students observe the pupils of their eyes by looking at a neighbor's eyes very closely. Have them note the size of the pupils. Then darken the room as much as you can. Have children close and shield their eyes with their hands to further avoid any light. (Tell them not to press on their eyes.)

After ten seconds, they should open their eyes, and watch each other's pupils. Are they the same size as before? Why is their size changing back to the way it was before they shut their eyes? What will their pupils be like on a bright day at the beach? What about in the movies?

The pupil regulates the amount of light energy entering the eye. The colored iris is a muscle which controls the pupils' size. When it is bright, the iris expands, cutting down the size of the pupil. When it is very dark, the iris pulls back and opens the pupil to allow more light energy to enter the eye.

What part of the ear is like a pupil? (The ear canal is the opening through which sound comes in, while the pupil allows light to come in.)

5. Why shouldn't people look directly at the sun? (No matter how well the iris and pupil work together, too much light will enter the eye and cause damage to it.)

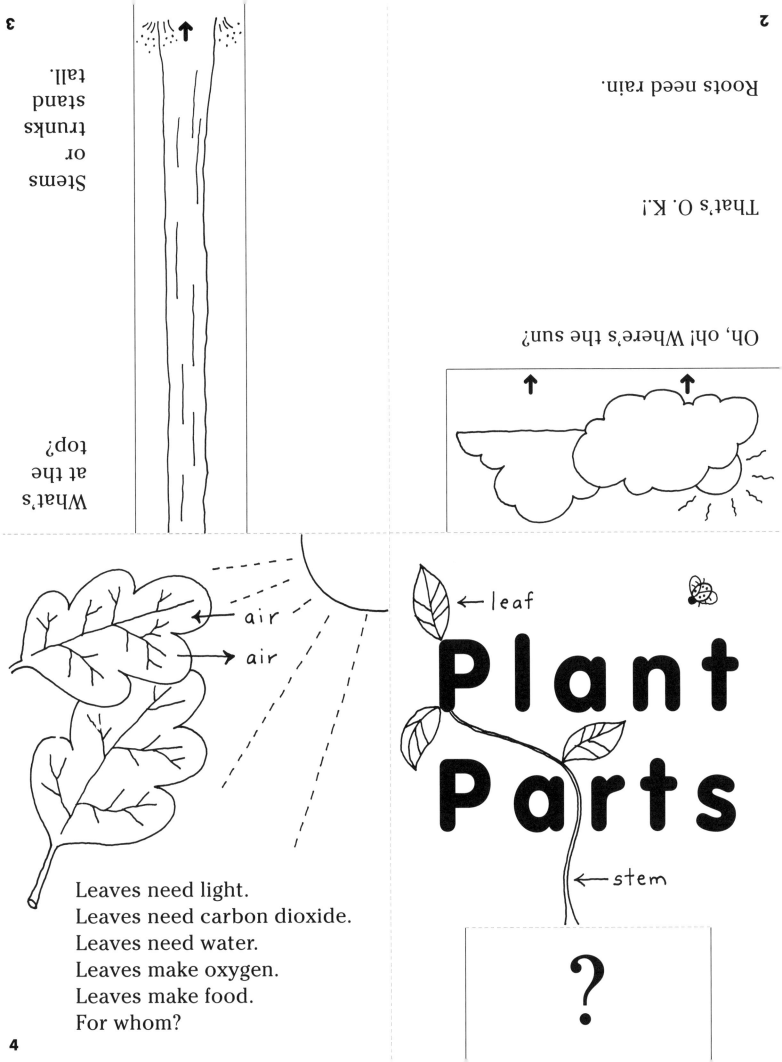

Stems or trunks stand tall.

What's at the top?

Roots need rain.

That's O. K.!

Oh, oh! Where's the sun?

Plant Parts

← leaf

← stem

?

air

air

Leaves need light.
Leaves need carbon dioxide.
Leaves need water.
Leaves make oxygen.
Leaves make food.
For whom?

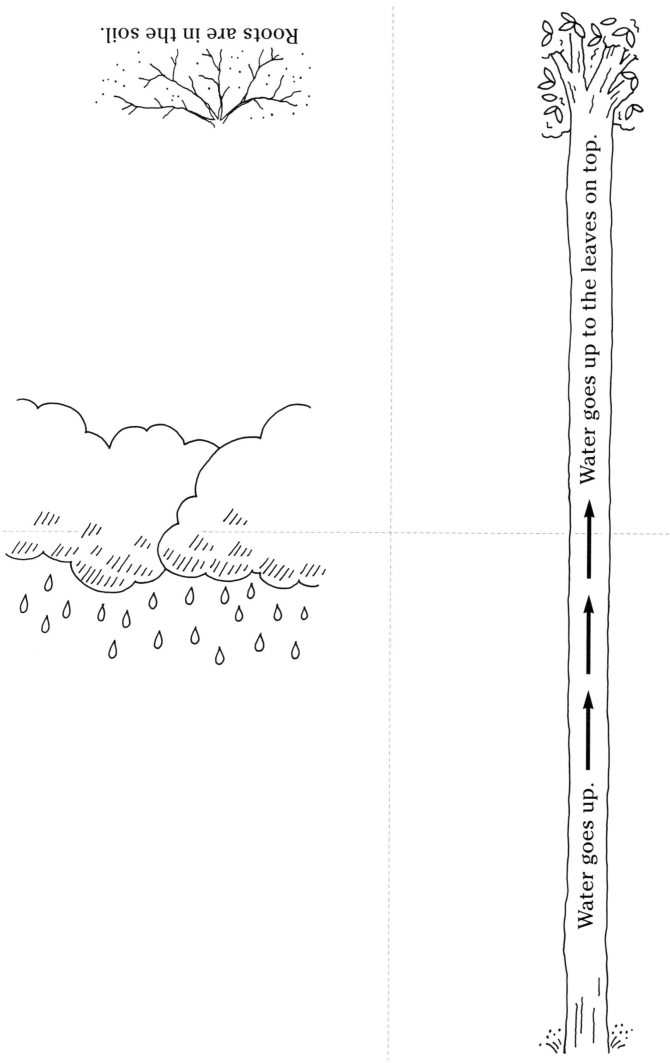

Roots are in the soil.

Water goes up to the leaves on top.

Water goes up.

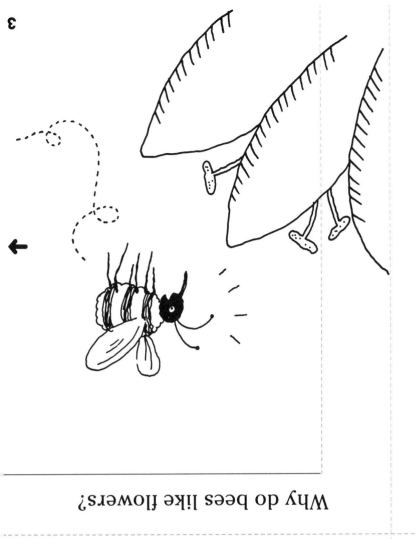

Why do bees like flowers?

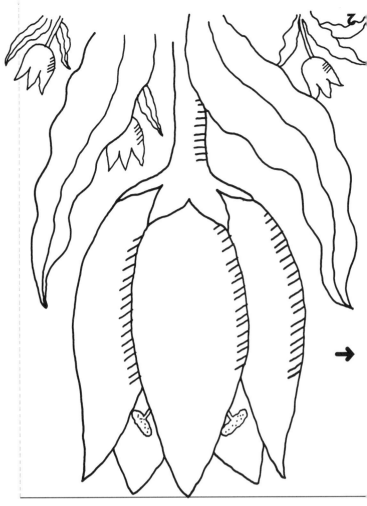

Pollen goes in the egg.
This makes a <u>seed</u>!

What are flowers for?
Flowers can make a

_____ _____ _____ _____ !

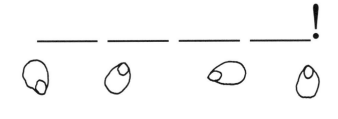

What are flowers for?

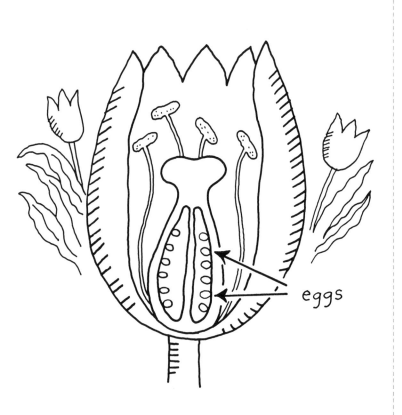

eggs

Inside are tiny eggs.

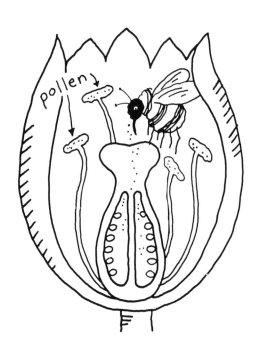

pollen

Bees get pollen for food.
Some pollen falls down to the egg.

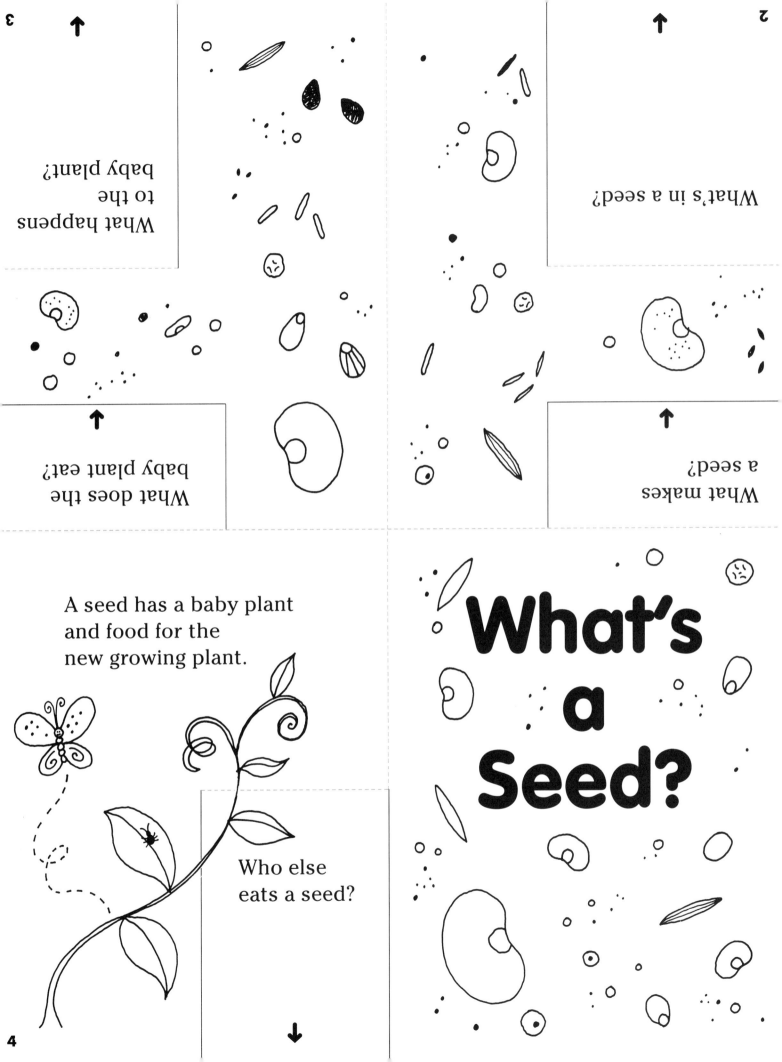

3

What happens to the baby plant?

What does the baby plant eat?

2

What's in a seed?

What makes a seed?

A seed has a baby plant and food for the new growing plant.

Who else eats a seed?

What's a Seed?

4

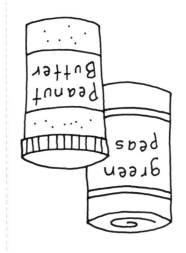

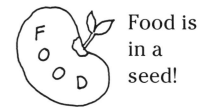

Food is
in a
seed!

A baby plant

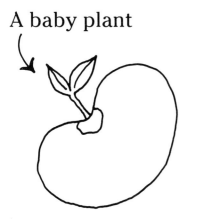

It grows!

In fall, birds eat fruit and drop the seeds. They help seeds go. Where?

In fall, wind helps seeds with wings or parachutes go. Where?

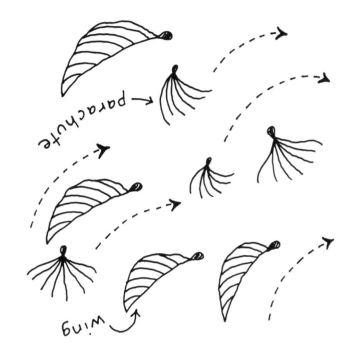

parachute

wing

Seed go!
They go to
get more sun!

They go to get
more rain.

They go to get more room in soil.
Why?

(unfold and open the page to see!)

Seeds on the Go!

In fall, squirrels help acorns go.
They hide them for food in spring.
Where?

In fall, animals and wind help seeds blow and go.
Soon spring's rain, sun, and soil can help them grow!

Who will help the new seeds go?
Can you guess? Do you know?

Lift to see.

Lift to see.

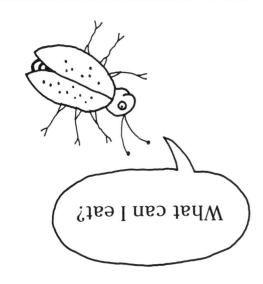

What can I eat?

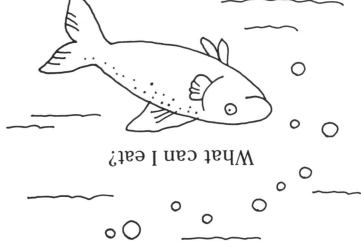

What can I eat?

But what do leaves eat?

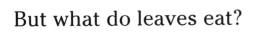

Lift leaf to see.

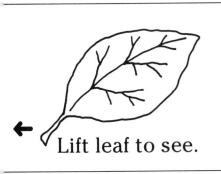

Fish can eat bugs.
Bugs can eat a leaf.
Plants make food to start

All living things need food.

4

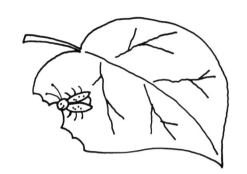

Leaves make their
food from water, and
carbon dioxide from
the air. Light helps
to make it. ☼

Fish can eat bugs.

Bugs can eat a leaf.

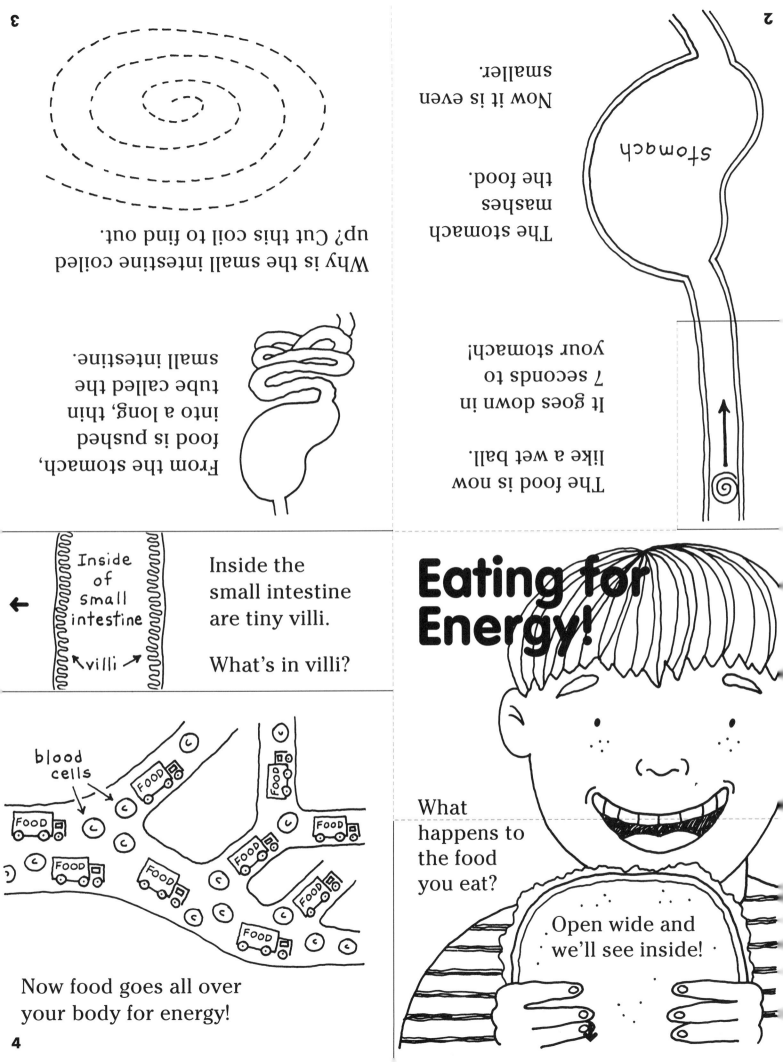

Why is the small intestine coiled up? Cut this coil to find out.

From the stomach, food is pushed into a long, thin tube called the small intestine.

stomach

Now it is even smaller.

The stomach mashes the food.

It goes down in 7 seconds to your stomach!

The food is now like a wet ball.

Inside
of
small
intestine

← villi →

Inside the small intestine are tiny villi.

What's in villi?

blood cells

FOOD

Now food goes all over your body for energy!

Eating for Energy!

What happens to the food you eat?

Open wide and we'll see inside!

Your
incisors
cut the
food.

Your
tongue
helps

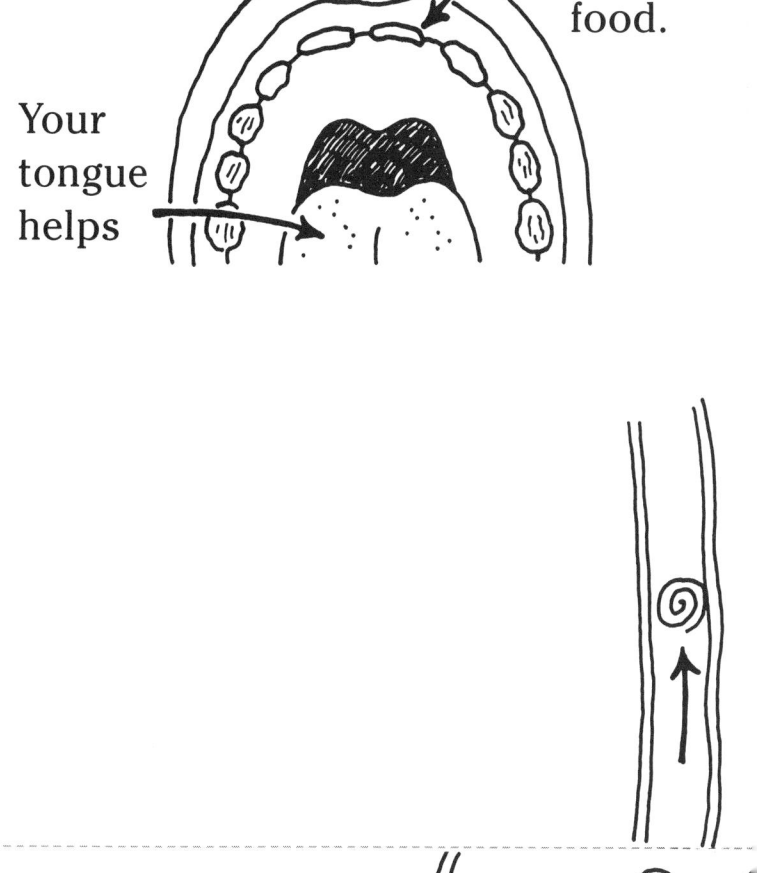

It wouldn't fit in your body
if it wasn't coiled up.
It's 20 feet long!
The food pieces get even smaller!

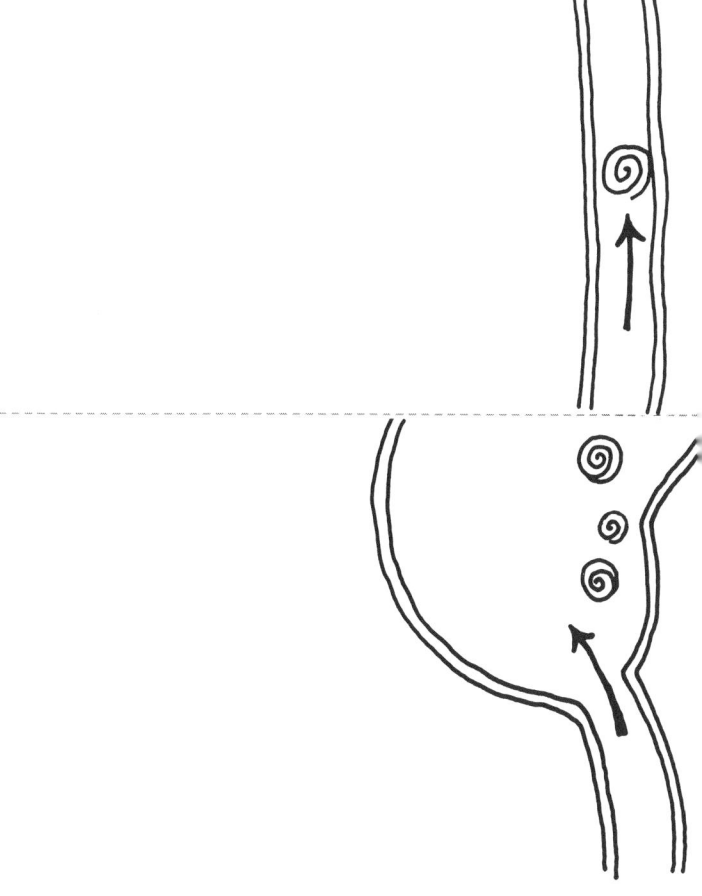

Food molecules go
into the blood there.

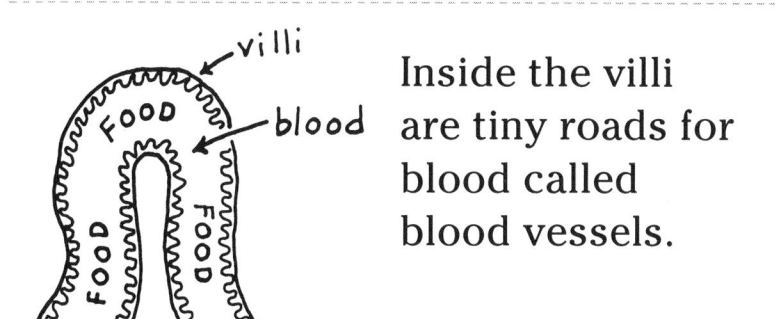

Inside the villi are tiny roads for blood called blood vessels.

push food down.

Teeth make big pieces into little pieces.

Molars have many points for grinding.

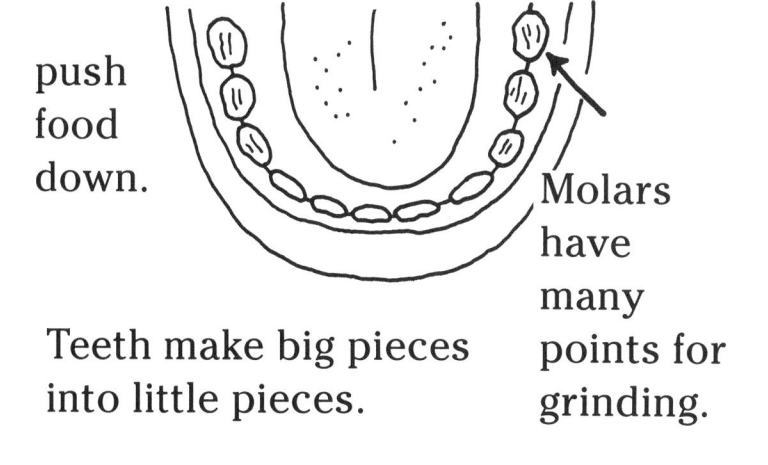

What are germs?

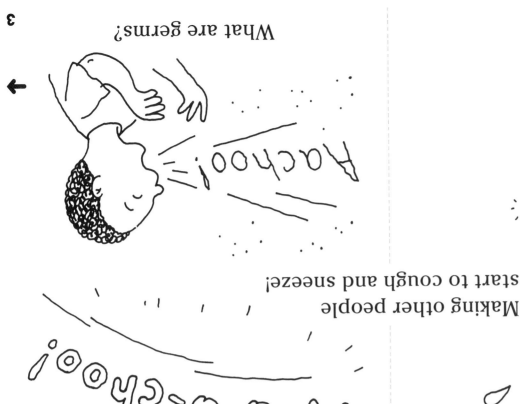

Aachoo!

Making other people
start to cough and sneeze!

A-a-a-choo!

choo!

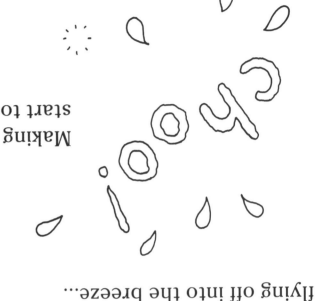

So germs don't go
flying off into the breeze...

Clean is Healthy!

SOAP + WATER
kills germs!

Clean is Healthy!

a·a·a·a

Cover your nose and mouth
when you cough or sneeze,

Germs can make you sick!

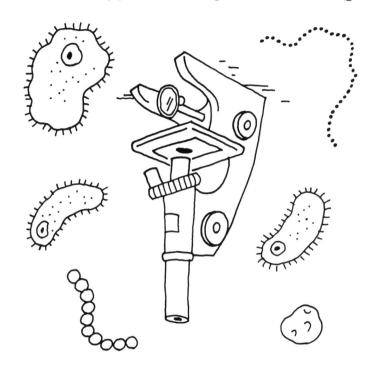

Germs are too little to see
without a microscope.

Your skin helps
to keep germs out.

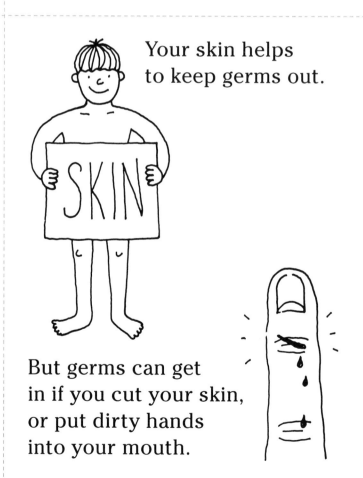

But germs can get
in if you cut your skin,
or put dirty hands
into your mouth.

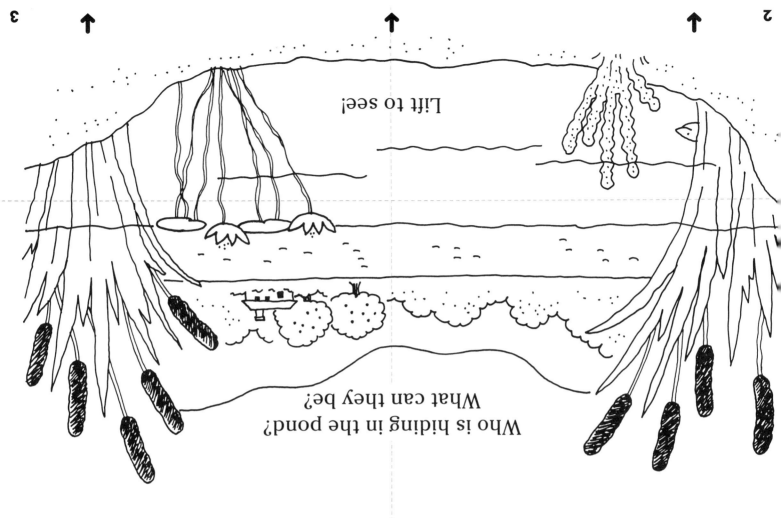

Lift to see!

Who is hiding in the pond?
What can they be?

Here you can see the birds, who are members of the Pond Community!

Birds with long beaks, neck and legs fish for dinner.

Ducks dive for crabs, insects and plants.

4

The Busy Pond

The busy pond has plants and animals you can or cannot see living together in a pond community!

dragonflies

turtles

frogs

water snake eating a frog

Many food chains are in the pondwater.
Big fish eat little fish and insects.
Little fish eat insects and plants.
Insects eat plants and littler fish.

water strider

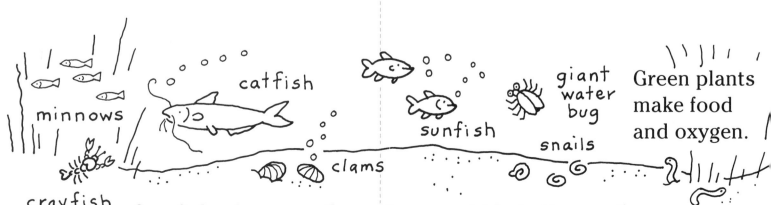

minnows

catfish

sunfish

giant
water
bug

snails

Green plants
make food
and oxygen.

clams

crayfish

worms

Crayfish, clams, snails, and worms hide in the mud!

The Job of Beaks

Wide beaks that look like saws can catch.

Pointy beaks make holes in trees.

Sharp beaks catch.

Short, thick beaks crack.

The Job of Feathers

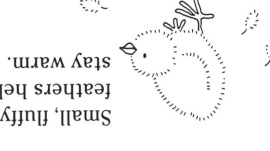

What bird has no flight feathers, only down feathers?

Small, fluffy down feathers help birds stay warm.

Flight feathers help birds push the air so they can fly.

quill

vane

The Job of Feet!

Webbed feet swim.

Sharp claws or talons catch animals.

Long legs wade in the water.

Reading a Bird!

You can learn to read a bird, almost like a book!
You won't see a printed word, just feet and beaks, and feathers—look!

Penguins live
where it's cold.
They don't fly.
They swim.
Down feathers
keep them warm!

seeds

animals

insects

fish and
plants

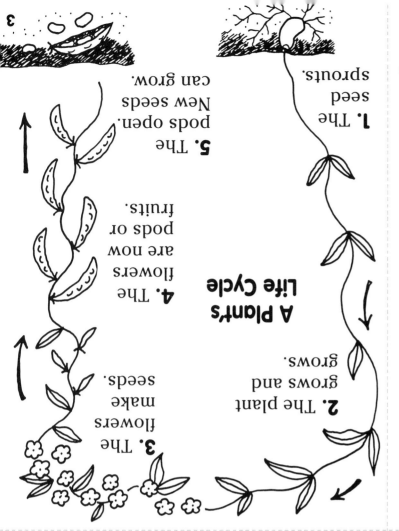

A Plant's Life Cycle

1. The seed sprouts.

2. The plant grows and grows.

3. The flowers make seeds.

4. The flowers are now pods or fruits.

5. The pods open. New seeds can grow.

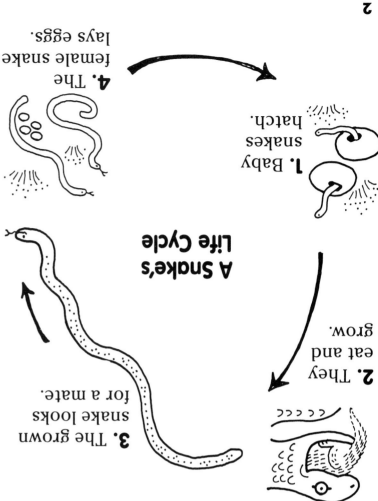

A Snake's Life Cycle

1. Baby snakes hatch.

2. They eat and grow.

3. The grown snake looks for a mate.

4. The female snake lays eggs.

 Birds lay eggs.

 Plants make seeds.

Human beings do not lay eggs or make seeds. We are born, eat and grow. We have a life cycle, too!

What is a Life Cycle?

1. The chick hatches.

2. Baby birds eat and grow.

3. The grown bird looks for a mate.

4. The female lays eggs.

Home is a

to a

To an

home is a

home is a

To a

Many animals agree
that for a home,
a tree
is a good place
to be!

web on a tree.

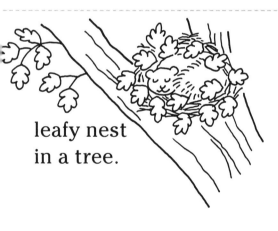

leafy nest
in a tree.

hole in
a tree.

3

brown brown brown brown brown brown brown

Color me brown.

← What am I?

2

green green green green green green green green green

Color me green.

→ What am I?

Hide and Seek

An Animal Coloring Game of Camouflage

Help the animals hide.

GAME RULES

↓

Color me brown and gray.

Color the sand brown and gray.

Who am I?

↓

4

Read the
color words.
Color the
animals.
Color the
background.

I'm a flounder,
hiding in
the sand.

I'm a grasshopper,
hiding in the grass.

I'm a mother
cardinal, hiding
with my eggs.

I just "hang out" during most of the day...

If I stayed in the daytime sun,
my skin would get dried out.
The nighttime moon
won't dry my skin—
that's when I splash about!

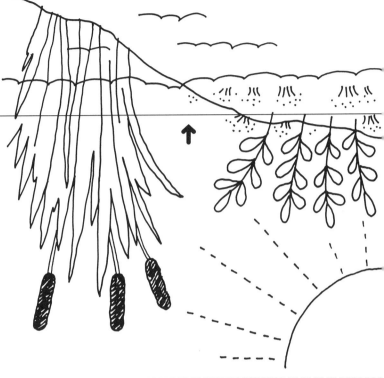

Nature at Night

Many animals are
busy at night while
you are fast asleep.
They are nocturnal.

Whoooo am I?

Cat

My shining eyes reflect the light,
so I see better in the night! Meow!

At night I use "radar" to catch my prey.

Mouse-eared Bat

My hearing helps me
catch my meal of mice,
even in the dark.
Mice don't hear or see me!

Leopard Frog

Barn Owl

I make a sound
that echoes back,
then I go in for
the attack!

← Answer 3

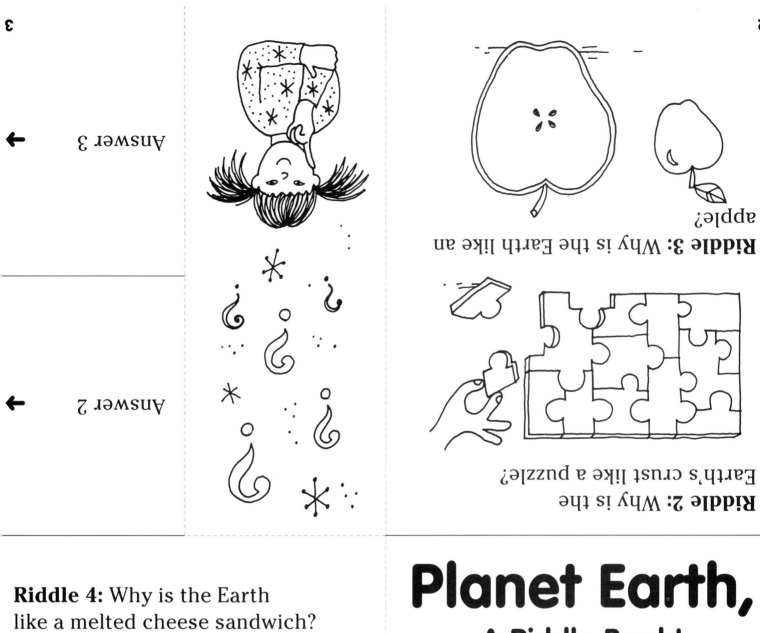

Riddle 3: Why is the Earth like an apple?

← Answer 2

Riddle 2: Why is the Earth's crust like a puzzle?

Riddle 4: Why is the Earth like a melted cheese sandwich?

Planet Earth,
A Riddle Book!

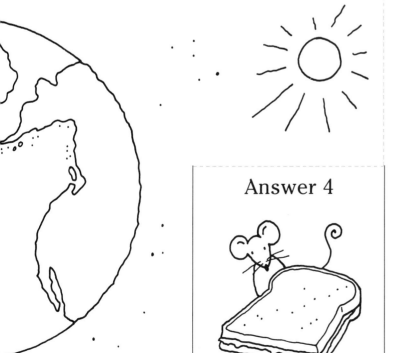

Answer 4

Riddle 1: Why is the Earth like a loaf of bread?

The inside
of the Earth
has a core.

The part under
the crust is
melted!
(Not cheese,
but rock!)
It is called
the mantle.

The Earth is covered
with crust.
We live on the thicker
parts called land.
The oceans cover the
thinner parts of the crust.

The crust is
made of big
pieces that
fit together.

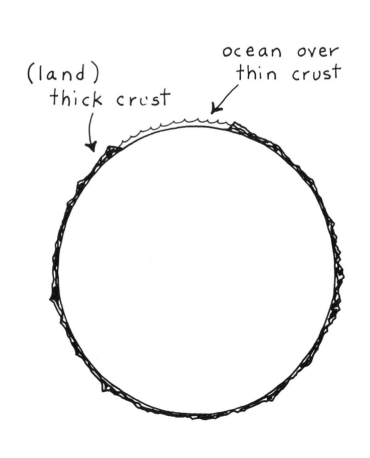

(land)
thick crust

ocean over
thin crust

The pieces
are called
plates.

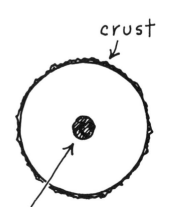

core

crust

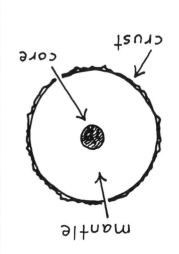

crust

core

mantle

Tall, young mountains become old, small, hills.

What happens to tall mountains when the wind and rain move soil away?

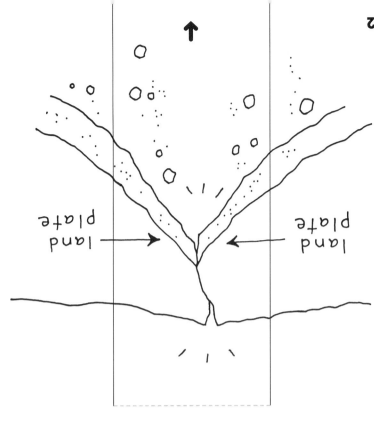

land plate

land plate

What happens when two plates of land BUMP together?

What happens when plates of land move apart?

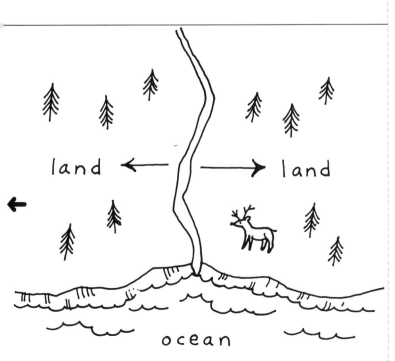

land ← → land

ocean

S-L-O-W
Changes on Earth

The earth is old. Its crust is cracked into pieces called plates.

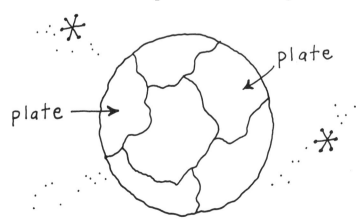

plate

plate

The plates move s-l-o-w-l-y!

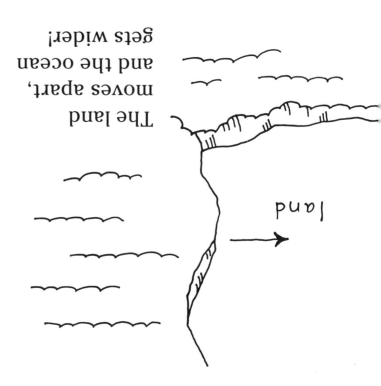

The land moves apart, and the ocean gets wider!

land

Tall mountains form!

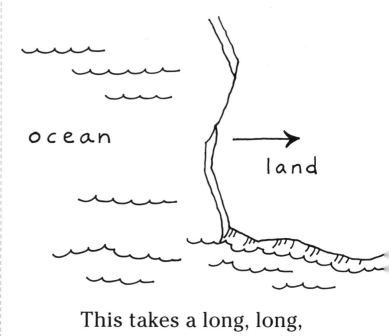

ocean

land

This takes a long, long, long, long, time!

Swinging, swinging, up so high,
You feel you can almost
touch the sky!
Will the swing keep going
round and round?

Climbing up
to the top
such a long,
long way,

Playing With Earth's Gravity!

Earth's gravity helps
you play ball.
Throw it up to a friend,
and down it will fall!

You can't see
Earth's gravity but
you can feel it.
When you jump up,
it can make you sit!

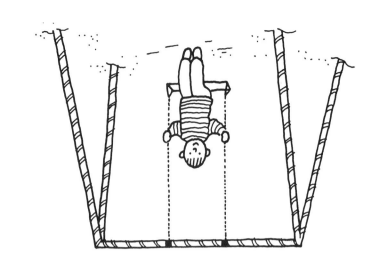

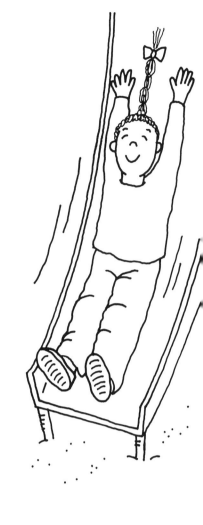

But sliding
back down
is just like play—
'cause gravity
pulls you
every day!

No, gravity
will pull you
back down to the
ground!

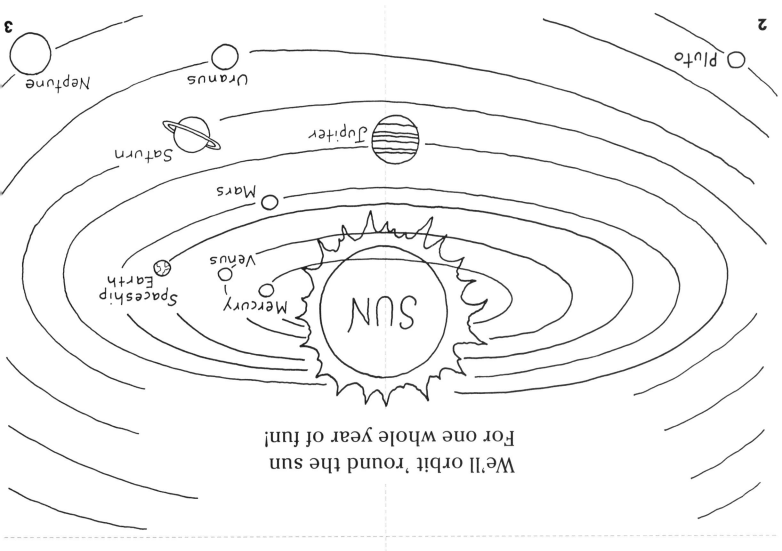

We'll orbit 'round the sun
For one whole year of fun!

It takes a whole year for Earth
to travel around the sun.
You'll have a "Happy Birthday"
each and every time
the trip is done!

A TRIP IN SPACE ON

How many trips have you had?
Draw the candles on the cake.

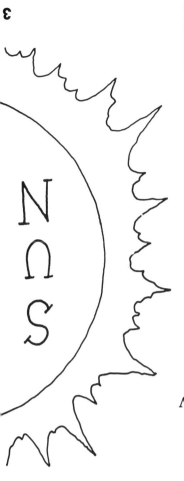

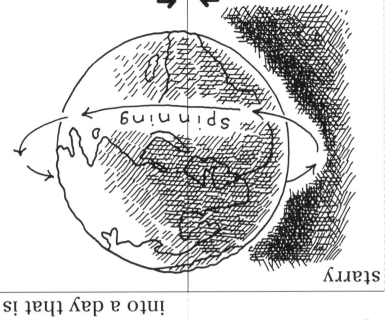

When the side that you're on now faces the light, stars fade away, into a day that is

When the side that you're on spins away from the light, sunny daytime becomes dark, starry

January 31	February 28¼	March 31
April 30	May 31	June 30
July 31	August 31	September 30
October 31	November 30	December 31

In 365 spins, so amazingly fast, for people on Earth, a whole year will have passed!

365 1/4 days = 1 year =

? months of spinning!

Take a SPIN on Planet Earth!

Every 24 hours (which is a full day) Our planet keeps on spinning in a very dizzy way!

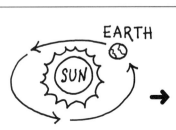

Besides going around the sun,

the Earth spins like a top!

night!

bright!

(In daytime, the stars are still there, but they blend into the sun's light!)

What do you think
this constellation is?

Who is this?

People used the stars
to tell stories.

The Little Dipper

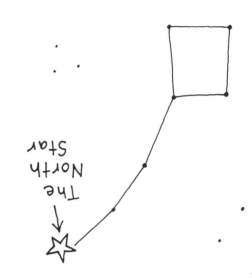

The North Star

People used the star patterns
to help find their way.

This is Draco the Dragon.

1 2

3

4

5

12

6

7

8   9   10   11

Is this
his
tongue?

Can you connect the dots
on his long tail?

Connect the
Dots!

A Starry Story
of
Constellations

This is Orion, the hunter.

This is Taurus, the bull.
Orion was hunting him.

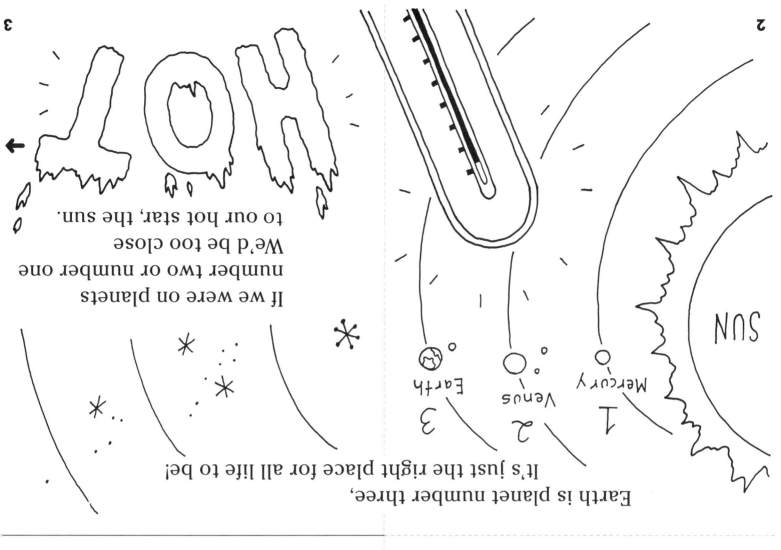

HOT

If we were on planets
number two or number one
We'd be too close
to our hot star, the sun.

SUN

Mercury 1

Venus 2

Earth 3

Earth is planet number three,
It's just the right place for all life to be!

Life lives on Earth,
that's Planet Number Three.
It's only place in the
solar system for life to be.

Yes, Earth's got life,
water, air and light,
Yes, Planet Number Three
is the place that's just right.

EARTH

PLANET
NUMBER THREE

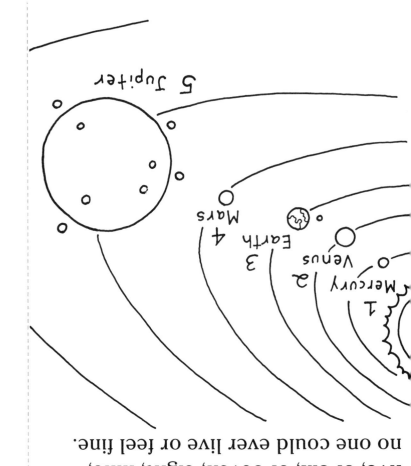

If we were way out on planets four,
five, or six, or seven, eight, nine,
no one could ever live or feel fine.

Not with the dark,
or the shivery cold—
Nothing could live there,
or ever grow old!

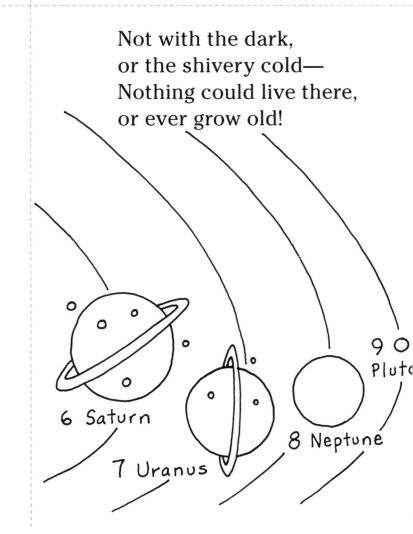

Big stars and planets are
so far away, they look like
without a telescope!

· · · · ·

You can't see little
germs even when
they are close.
With a microscope,
they look...

Aaachoo!

Little or big, all
things take up room.

Big or little,
all things are matter.

Do you take up room?

Then you are

m-___-___-___-r!

Big
and little
Matter!

little dots

big!

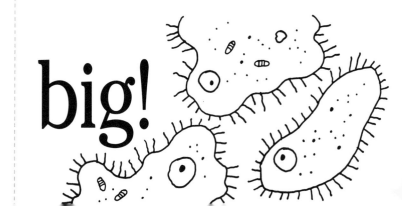

← a GAS

or

← a LIQUID

or

← a SOLID

or

Matter can be . . .

When you have many molecules you can make big things.

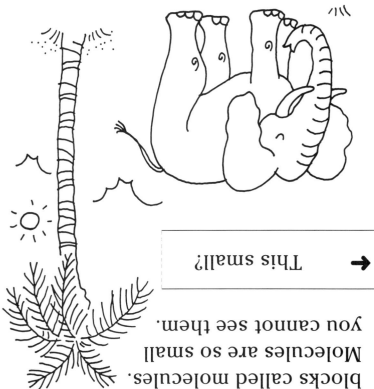

→ This small?

Molecules are so small you cannot see them.

All matter is made of tiny building blocks called molecules.

You can stand
on a solid chair.
This matter holds you
because the molecules
hold each other
close together.

But,
don't stand on the air!

Air is a gas.
Its molecules are too far apart.

The Why You Can Stand On a Chair, But Not On the Air Book!

All things that take
up room are matter.

Chairs take up room
in a room.

You take up room
on a chair because
you are matter.
What else is matter?

Smaller than a · !

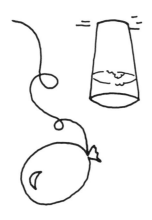

Milk takes up room
in a cup.

Air takes up room
in a balloon.

Molecules in solids
are very close together.
They hold tight.
Solid matter keeps its shape.

Molecules in liquids
are not as close together.
Liquid matter can move and splash.

 or

Molecules in a gas
are very far apart.
A gas has <u>no</u> shape.

↑

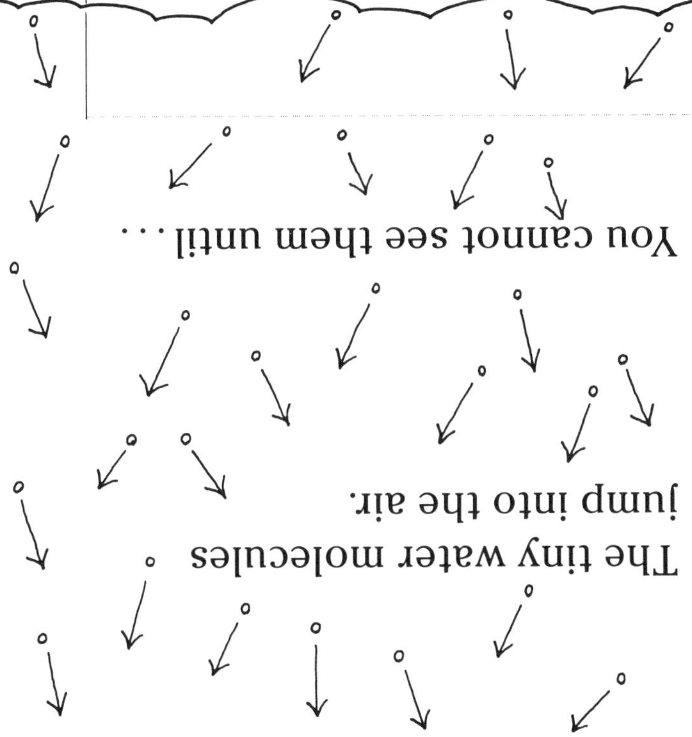

You cannot see them until . . .

The tiny water molecules jump into the air.

↑

The sun warms the water.

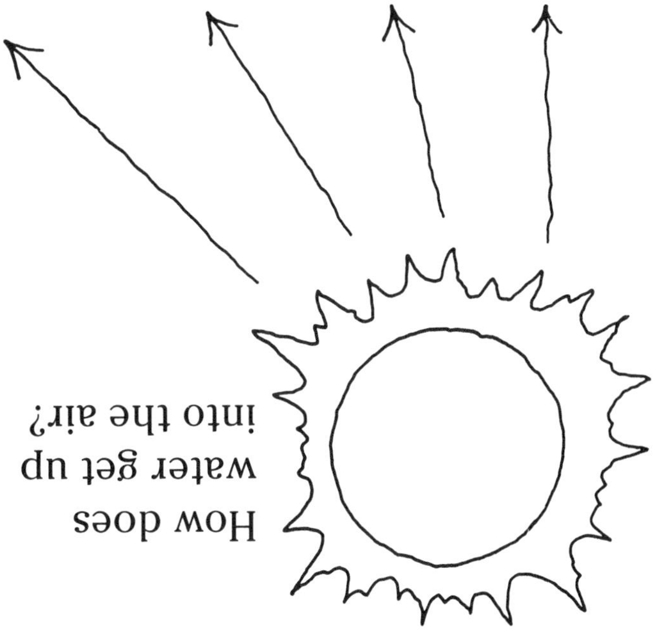

How does water get up into the air?

What is in gray clouds?

When the water droplets get too big, they drop!

The water goes into puddles, lakes, and oceans.

What makes the clouds again?

The

Why is this a water cycle?

Clouds or the Water Cycle

Clouds are made of water.

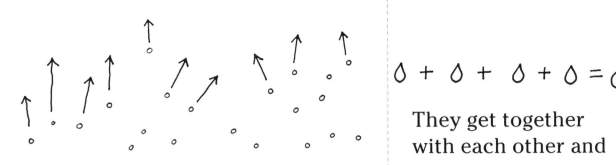

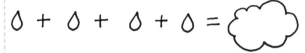

They get together
with each other and

Something that
happens over
and over again.

Gray clouds
have lots
of water.

What's a cycle?

Little bits of water
called molecules get hot.
This makes them jump.

make water droplets
in a cloud.

Where does the
sound go next?

The sound goes in a tunnel
called the ear canal.

When the vibrating air comes near,
your outer ears catch its sound.

Sound goes into your ear canal,
and travels to your brain. Put your
finger on the ear canal below, and
follow it to the brain. Your brain
tells you what you hear.

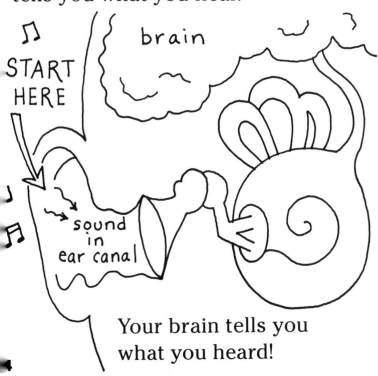

START
HERE

brain

sound
in
ear canal

Your brain tells you
what you heard!

HEARING SOUNDS

Songs

Sound energy happens when
molecules VIBRATE.

What's that?

Air molecules are too tiny to see, but your ears feel them move.

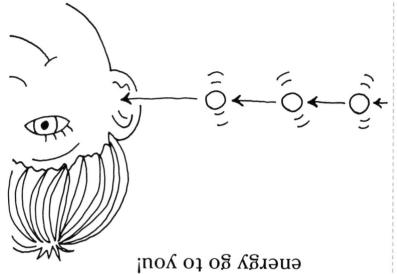

Each air molecule vibrates and makes the next one shake. This make the sound energy go to you!

When the bell rings, it vibrates or shakes. The shaking bell makes the air molecules shake.

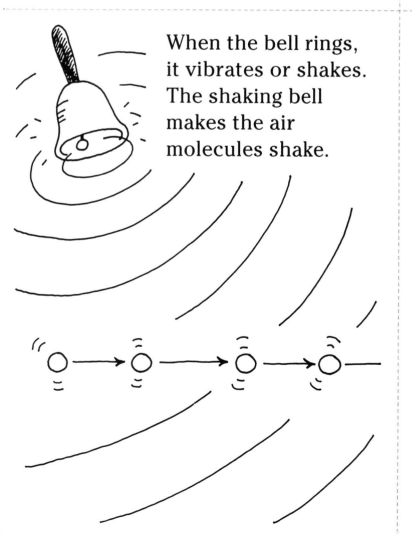

Light goes in the window.
What does the light change to?
Open the door to find out.

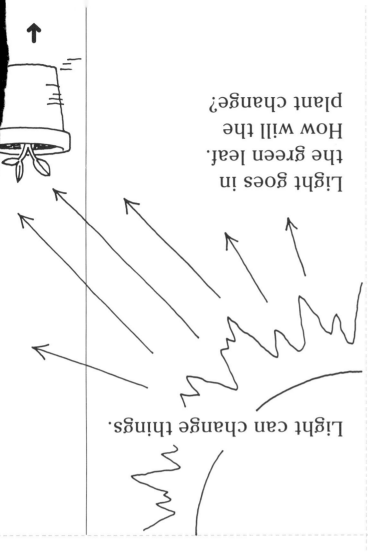

Light goes in
the green leaf.
How will the
plant change?

Light can change things.

Light from
the sun
can change.

LIGHT

Light comes from the sun.
Sunlight is white.
But what is white light?

White light goes in. What will
come out?

glass prism ?

Light is energy.
We need
light energy
so we
can

Hey, turn on the light!

Just open the door!

White light is
made of colors!

Light can
change into
heat energy.

see!

The
leaf
mak
food
The
plant
will
grow.

We feel
so hot!

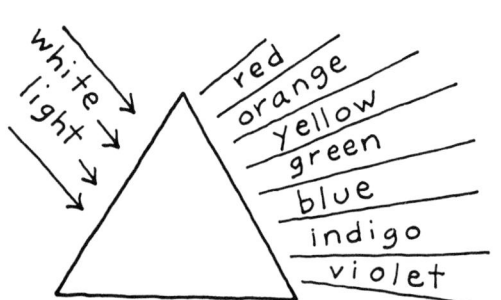

The prism
broke the
white
light up!

Use your crayons to show what
color white light is made of!

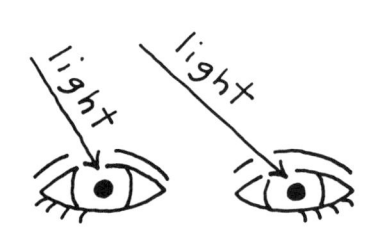

Light goes
into the
pupil of
your eye,
so you
can see.